Uncle Ed Said

Ed Davidson

Growing Up

During the Great Depression

In Ontonagon, Michigan

AP

AMERICAN
PERSPECTIVE
Ltd

American Perspective, Ltd.
6191 Cowell Road
Brighton, MI 48116
877/711-1229

Preface

My mother Eleanore never spoke much about growing up in Ontonagon, Michigan during the depression. There were stories my sister and I liked to hear about the cow that, upon being released from its small barn at the end of winter, would jump and gambol about the yard celebrating its freedom; but the other stories she told about rabbit stew and snow piled higher than houses were told with a sense of relief that those times were well past.

When my mom passed away, her siblings, Delilah, Arlene and Ed, spent time with my father and me. They had a chance to talk with and comfort each other and started remembering the stories of their youth. There were tales of love and loss, of poverty, and the long hours of work that were required from everyone in the family.

But there were also stories about chewing the same stick of gum for days and saving it on the bedpost overnight because it was such a delectable luxury, or the remembrance of eating a rich buttery Ritz cracker for the first time at a friend's house and thinking it was the tastiest cracker in the world.

It would be nice, I thought, if I could gather these stories into a book so that our descendents could appreciate the rich heritage and determination of these first generation Finnish-Americans. I really didn't know if they had the time to undertake such a project. I said I'd help in any way I could.

And then Uncle Ed sent me some stories. They were the stories of life and work during the depression in

Ontonagon, Michigan. They weren't filled with bitterness over their poverty or tales of hunger and desperation.

They were stories of hope and belief, hard work and improvisation. They were stories about my Grandpa Emil driving a car without a heater, rubbing the inside of the windshield with a bag of salt as he drove, and Grandma Impi scrubbing the floors of the one room schoolhouse on her hands and knees.

Eleanore, Impi and Uncle Ed

They were hopeful stories of struggle, triumph, friendship and neighbors.

It was a hard life. They were a family of inventors, recyclers, and innovators. Anything useful was repurposed before it was discarded. What food they couldn't produce on their land came from the forests and rivers. Uncle Ed explains how they did it.

But there's no whining in these stories, no sense that life had been unfair, or that God had stacked the deck against them.

They are stories many immigrant families lived, surviving together, making the best of their chosen country, America.

My son Eliot and I transcribed the stories and put them in book form from Uncle Ed's handwritten pages, but we made every effort to keep the words just as they were written.

Uncle Ed and me, 1953

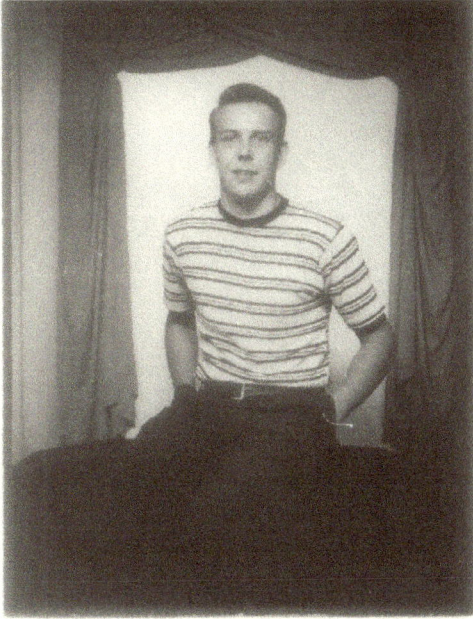

Foreword
"Wayne has asked me several times to put down on paper some interesting happenings and events of our past life in the U.P. I was reminded the other day of a story which will give you some idea of travel and transportation in those days."

That's how this all started. That's what Uncle Ed said.

About Our Automobiles

When my grandparents first homesteaded the area there were no roads – they hiked into their places and built their houses, barns, etc., and the more affluent people had a team of horses to clear the land and eventually work the soil on their farms. Surprisingly, it was only a matter of a few years when one could see fields of grain and hay emerge out of the forests. Now they could grow potatoes and other vegetables as well as fruit trees. There were many species of wildlife to be had so now their survival was assured and firewood could be sold in town for cash, sugar, coffee, flour and kerosene. Pretty much everything else was acquired by their own labor. Every farm that was of any size had a blacksmith shop with a forge to create tools for the farm such as tongs, plow shares, grub hoes, etc. They were mostly all good at woodworking, making their own axe handles, whipple sticks for the teams, sleighs for hauling, wagons and on and on.

During this point in time they gradually built roads connecting their farms and a horse trail into town. There were many rivers and creeks so there were a lot of bridges to build also. The winter time saw lots of horse and sleigh traffic but in the spring when the frost was gone the roads remained impassable because there weren't any ditches, nor was there any gravel. The trails were a sea of mud much of the summer. When the first Model T's began to appear they would sometimes drive through the fields near the road because the roads were so bad.

In another ten or twenty years things were a lot better. The farms were larger and there was grain as well as produce, milk, meat, and firewood to sell so progress was made. About the same time the prohibition era came along so there were a lot of "bootleggers" making and selling spirits. We had a neighbor who would go across the border to Wisconsin and buy a load of booze and sell it to the local Gentry. On one of his trips he was coming back about 1 A.M. and decided to stop at a small diner to have some coffee. Too late he saw a State Police car parked outside the place and the trooper was just leaving. Dick had a '36 Chevrolet coupe and the trunk was loaded with cases of whiskey making the car sag nearly to the ground. Well, when he pulled up the trooper immediately called him over and said, "What have you got in your car making the back end sag so low?" Dick replied, "What the hell do you think I have? It's filled with booze." The cop looked at him, shook his head and said, "I hate smart asses," got in his patrol car and left.

Before long everyone had a car, all Model T Fords. The roads were made wider and the county purchased a rock crusher and most were graveled and ditched so it slowly got to be a more mobile society and traffic grew heavier by the year. Then around the early 30's there were several companies producing automobiles, so even in this remote part of the country people were trying all these new cars with clutches and transmissions. Most were now "closed" so you didn't need side curtains – a plus in snow country. As an example, I'll tell of one neighbor's vehicle he owned while we lived there. He tried all different brands. The first was a '27 Ford roadster pick-up, then came a '35 Dodge coupe, a '28 Studebaker (a big straight 8), a '35 Nash twin ignition job – also I forgot in between he had a '29 Durant and a '32

Essex Super Six – a '29 Ford coupe and a '37 Ford 60 h.p. (kind of a mini car). When we moved away he had a '41 Ford, so there were a lot of brands available.

I tried to remember what each family had when I was a kid. One had a '31 Reo, another had a '29 Oakland, '27 Oldsmobile, '25 Olds Touring 4 door, '27 Buick Opera coupe… Emil Jussila was a little man and he bought a Rickenbacker (I don't know what year) and he looked like a midget driving it. It was huge. My first car, which was my own at age 11, was a '29 Whippet – almost a twin to the Durant. Some were really big loads of iron. A car called Flint was so big and rigid they advertised that if you removed any wheel it would remain in an upright position,

Uncle Ed's 1929 Model A

standing on three wheels. The Erskine was a nice small car, I think made by Chrysler. A friend of ours had a '29 Nash, another giant. Earlier he had an Auburn. I visited someone

11

while in Ontonagon on vacation around 1987 and he said "Come out. I want to show you something." We went out to a shed behind the barn and he opened the door. Inside was a '29 air-cooled Franklin in mint condition. He had found it at someone's farm and bought it for $35.

A funny story was that when Ford came out with the V-8 engine, that was what they were called. You never heard that someone had a Ford, they said he got a new V-8. Well, one day the news was out that Heikkila had a new car, so all the men from the area rushed over to have a look at it. When we got there he was standing proudly beside his new Oakland coupe – it was a black beauty. One person asked him what it was and he said, "It's an Oakland." Well, another guy was looking under the hood and said, "Oh, it's a V-8." Heikkila said, "No, it's an Oakland." But the guy persisted and said, "Yes, but it's still a V-8." At this point Heikkila got irate and said, "Dammit! It's an Oakland, not a V-8. I'll show you the title." The discussion got more heated and they had to restrain them both or there would have been a real battle.

Some people said not to ever buy a V-8 because the pistons are lying on their sides and wear out right away on one side.

Another funny story was that a guy we called Heiki lived at the bottom of a big hill on the river bank. He bought a '26 Model T. One day a bunch of us walked down to the river to go fishing. Heiki was outside so we stopped and talked to him. One of the guys asked him how he liked his new Ford. He said it was a really good car and he loved it.

We asked him if it had enough power to climb the steep hill leaving his house. He said, "Yes. It isn't any problem. I just keep it in second gear and it goes right up."

12

Well Johnny said, "A Model T doesn't have a second gear. They only have a low and high gear." He replied, "I put it in low and keep my right foot on the brake to hold it back some. That's second." Oh well!

In later years many of these old cars were made into "Bugs". The body was removed and sometimes the drive shaft to make it shorter. Many times another transmission was installed in tandem with the original giving a real low gear ratio and increasing the power about 100%. They were old Buicks and Nashes and mostly six or eight cylinders were used. They made powerful cheap tractors.

I have a picture of a creation made by someone who mounted a Model T engine, transmission and radiator on 2 x 4's on a raft with a large airplane type propeller. I don't think they'd have enough RPM's to drive it very fast and I wonder if it worked at all.

Many old cars had a rear fender knocked off and they'd throw a belt over the tire and run a circular saw to cut firewood. This was a common sight before the chainsaw.

When I worked in the lumber camp a friend bought a '29 Hudson, another hulk like a locomotive. When we were ready to go home I said I'd wait and see if it got started. He went outside and hand cranked it for about 5 minutes. It was about -20°. Then he threw the crank in the back seat, hit the starter and it fired up. The next day I asked him why he cranked it when the starter worked. He said, "I always do that to loosen it up so the starter doesn't have to work so hard!"

Our neighbors had a "Bug" made from a '24 Oldsmobile and when it was first cut down it had 4,000 miles on it. The last time I saw it, it showed 88,000. All those miles were put on in the field, raking and mowing

Plowing with a Model A

hay over a period of many, many years. It had been overhauled many, many times but was a strong runner. The only trouble I remember was it had an open drive shaft and the hay would wrap around it so tight it would come to a complete stop. They'd have to take a knife out and cut away the hay. Later they mounted a long steel trough the length of the shaft to keep the hay off it.

The Furniture Movers

I was preparing to go to the U.P. on a deer hunting trip, and dad's brother Bill was down on a visit so he had called me and asked if he could have a ride back with me, and of course I agreed. I picked him up in Metamora and we started on our way. He talked a lot and always had interesting stories so I liked to pick his brain and get him started. This is exactly as I remember it and I haven't any reason to add or delete anything he said.

His and dad's sister Lydia and her husband Bart lived in Detroit and had recently decided to relocate back to the Copper Country and decided to settle in Laurium near Calumet. The year, as near as I can determine, was about 1924. Bart came to Ontonagon knowing Bill had a Model T Ford stake truck (I think a 1921). He persuaded Bill to drive to Detroit to pick up their furniture, so when they had agreed on a price, tuned the engine, and loaded all the gear, tools, spare parts and everything they thought would be needed, the two of them set out.

The roads back then weren't paved and they didn't even use much gravel, so when it rained there was an ocean of mud. Also, the only passable routes were between the biggest cities; for example from Mackinaw to Detroit the road traveled along Lake Huron through Oscoda, Alpena, Bay City, etc., adding perhaps 100 miles to the route traveled today.

Bill said the trip was uneventful and except for a few minor problems with the truck it all went quite well. I asked what the minor problems were and he said, *"Well, the truck ran okay but overheated a lot, so I was wondering what it* would be like coming back with a big load. We had several cans of gas and a few water cans because we had anticipated the engine overheating. The Model T didn't come with a water pump as a usual part of the equipment. Of course we needed extra gas because in those days there weren't many filling stations anywhere. Also, the Ford had a ten gallon tank and pistons that were like gallon pails so there weren't any miles per gallon records broken. We had driven for several hours and were somewhere east of Marquette when I told Bart 'This will never work,' so I pulled off the road into a nice grassy field.

I got the tool box out and started to dismantle the rear axle. I carried a set of high speed gears with me so while Bart took a nap I installed them and what a difference it made (He probably got it up to 30 m.p.h. now!)

We were going along real good and just as we neared the Seney Swamp we hit a thunderstorm. The truck had an open cab and I didn't have the right canvas roof or side curtains. I just tied a piece of canvas to each corner of the windshield and back to the stakes on the platform behind the front seat. It kind of worked, but we were soaked in a few minutes. There was only one windshield wiper on the driver's side and it had a handle that had to be operated back and forth by hand. I had my hands full trying to keep up the momentum because if we stopped we would have sunk right down to the hubs in mud. I yelled at Bart to grab the wiper so there we were – Bart leaning over manipulating the wiper as fast as he could and I hanging on to the wheel as we slid around in the deep ruts, rain pouring down and mud flying in all directions, including the cab. We were stuck real bad only 4 or 5 times and as soon as we got to more stable ground we decided to stop for the night and give it another shot in the morning.

We were up at daylight so we built a fire and got a coffeepot started. We were on a little logging road just forty or so feet off the main road. I spotted a couple rabbits nearby so I reached in the trunk and grabbed the shotgun and we had a nice breakfast before getting underway. We didn't see more than a half dozen cars on the way to St. Ignace. There weren't very many houses on that route so except for several teams of horses working in logging camps, and of course a lot of wild life, it was quite desolate.

We drove on the ferry boat to cross the Straits of Mackinac and the attendant took one look at the truck and said, 'Where the hell did you dig that thing up from?'

The rest of the way wasn't too bad. We had four flat tires and had to stop and adjust the coil points and clean the plugs a couple times. (The Model T didn't have a distributor. It had four coils, one for each cylinder. The points on each coil operated as interrupters for the spark coming from the timer to the spark plugs. It also had a magneto on the flywheel to supply the spark so there wasn't any battery for the ignition.)

We were now halfway and it was nice to have a break and get rested and look forward to starting home.

Before loading up and preparing for the return trip I decided to install new piston rings thinking it would provide a little more power for the heavy load going back.

After resting up for a week or so we began loading the furniture. There were five rooms plus all the clothing, dishes, etc. and we really had to pack it tight to fit it all in. (I estimate the size of that truck platform wasn't more than 7' x

9' so there was only one way to go. Up!) *When we were done we had a high, heavy load and I now am reminded of the truck in the TV show "The Beverly Hillbillies". We had a large canvas lashed tightly all around to keep the rain out. We had a flap right behind the front seat where we could crawl in and be covered, and left an opening large enough to lie down and sleep at night.*

After I had installed the new rings and tightened up the rods the engine really ran hot for about the first day until it began to even out. We stopped several times to fill our water cans and let it cool but it got better as we moved ahead. At one point it got really hot and we discovered the fan belt had broken. It was just a flat strap to turn the fan only so I took my belt off and measured it for size. I cut it the right length and punched holes in each end and tapped our supply of hay wire and weaved the two ends together. As far as I know it's still on the truck working perfectly. The only problem was my belt. I again went to our supply and cut off a piece of rope and tied it around my waist and just tied a knot in front. It kept my trousers up real good.

The Model T had a transmission that was probably the forerunner of all automatics ever since. There was a low band and it would automatically slip into high gear after getting underway. There was no clutch. The only problem was that high gear didn't have power enough and every hill large or small you had to go to low gear and that was about 10 mph tops. On level ground you had to go full bore so you'd have a little momentum to carry past the hill. There was no accelerator pedal. There was a handle on the steering column and that was usually in the wide open

18

position. So along with the crank there were a few differences in driving then and now.

A few days later we were on our way about 75 miles south of the Straits of Mackinac and had stopped for the night. We checked the truck and got set for the next day, made a fire and fixed supper right near Lake Huron. It was getting late so we both crawled under the tarp and fell asleep instantly. It was pitch dark and quiet except for a few ripples from the waters. Suddenly Bart gave me a punch and whispered that someone was coming. Sure enough, a couple of minutes later he heard a couple of men nearing our truck. The Model T didn't have a fuel pump so the gas tank was under the dash board and a pipe going down to the carb with gravity feed. The filler cap was right in front of the windshield. They began to open the filler cap with intentions of using a siphon and can to steal our gas. We of course were on top of the load above the cab. I silently stuck the barrel of the shotgun over their heads and squeezed off a round. That old 10 gauge shot a flame 4 feet long and sounded like a 105 howitzer. About five seconds of silence and then panic. Those guys must have thought it was Judgment Day. We heard them screaming and crashing through the brush and cranking up their 'T' and the last we heard of them was the whine of their engine screaming through the trees. Bart said we'd better leave or get ready in case they came back. I turned over and said 'They're long gone. We'll never see them again.'

With sunrise we got up and crawled out of our "bed" cautiously looking around but there wasn't anything or anyone around. Bart got down first and laughed as he found a gas can and piece of hose near the truck. A little farther, he found a man's shoe. The thief was in such a hurry he ran out of his shoes. That wasn't the last of it. A short distance away there on the ground was a set of false teeth. They must have really been running for their lives!

The next couple days went by without problems and we crossed on the ferry again and sure enough when we got near Seney Swamp the rains came again. This time our truck was much heavier so we really got mired. At one point we were stuck so bad we had to corduroy the road. (Corduroy is when you cut trees in eight or ten foot lengths and lay them side by side crossways making a stable footing to drive on.) *In order to get the wheels started on the new footing we had to raise them up and that was no easy problem. We cut a 4" tree about 10' long and used it as a lever to pry the wheel up and get it going on the new surface. By the next day we were on a road close to Lake Superior and the ground was sandy. We made good progress for about the next 50 miles.*

We had only one more section of really bad road. We came to a long steep hill and there must have been a spring about halfway down. We stopped and walked up there for a look and decided we wouldn't attempt going up there. There was mud and water knee deep and it would be impossible with our load. We opted to go through a farmer's field thinking our chances there were better than the muddy road. I swung into the field and started climbing the hill and nearly made it when the wheels started to spin and again we were really mired. I told Bart we'd never get up there without a tow and he agreed. I said I'd walk to the next farm and get help. I got to the owner and explained our situation. He listened and said 'Okay, I'll get the car and pull you out.' I said we'd need a team of horses but he said, 'No, I'll get you out'. He walked to the barn and got a heavy logging chain and proceeded to go down to the garage to the car. Again I protested and he said, 'Let's do it my way,' kind of sarcastically. I thought, okay, we'll see. He opened the garage door and backed his car out. It was an old Nash and looked like a boxcar. It was much bigger than my truck.

He backed up and hooked the chain on and we both gunned our engines and away he went - with my front axle and wheels. I'm left sitting in the mud while the whole front end was on the chain on his Nash.

Bart and I worked a day and a half putting our truck together again. A lot of baling wire and ingenuity and we were back on the road. Only one more ordeal before we got home. We were going along at a good clip and came upon a long steep hill. It was probably the heavy load or the weak brakes but we were going down fast. At the bottom was a hairpin turn which we must have taken at 50 mph. I desperately turned the corner wondering if we would tip over but the only thing that happened was that both front tires flew off and wrapped around the axle. I didn't know it before but that was a common problem with 30 x 3 ½" tires.

Finally we came to Houghton and I was thinking about crossing the bridge to Hancock and then climbing the Quincy Hill but the low band on the transmission was slipping badly and might not pull us up the hill. We got about half way up and got to the steep part and the Ford wouldn't go any further. Bart said, 'We're only twelve miles from home and now we're stuck!' I said, 'Not yet.'

Another common Model T problem was exactly what happened here. What do you do when you're stuck on a hill? Easy, you simply turn around and go up in reverse!

Everything ended up fine and we got home okay, furniture and all."

After Bill finished his story I thought about it awhile and asked him, "How much did he pay you for that trip?" I almost fell over when he said, "He promised to pay me $35, but that s.o.b. never gave me a cent."

The Military Hill Incident

One of the main roads coming into Ontonagon County is Highway U.S. 45. It begins in Mobile, Alabama and runs straight north, ending in Ontonagon. It is said that Abraham Lincoln had it built during the Civil War to give the slaves a direct route north and, for the Union Army, a way south. When it was built it was nearly all through wilderness and there were very few settlements on its course. If you were to travel it today, you would find a nearly direct line north passage with few deviations. That means it crossed rivers and continued on in a straight line. That being said, when the road crew neared Rockland, Michigan (about twelve miles south of Ontonagon) they came to the Ontonagon River. There were solid rock banks on both sides rising about 100 feet above the water. It seemed impossible to penetrate and, for whatever reason, they probably couldn't find a better spot to build a bridge. They went ahead and constructed a bridge and blasted a road through the rock. It was known then, and now, as the Military Hill. It curved straight down to the river and again straight up the other side, about three-quarters of a mile in both directions. Anyone who ever drove over it talked about it the rest of their lives. It was a sheer drop with a couple of sharp turns on both sides. There were signs posted on both sides to slow to ten miles per hour and use the low gear to go up or down. I still don't know how anyone could cross it in the winter with the old model cars of the day, even with tire chains.

Years later, when I moved to Detroit, I drove a semi for New Era (now Frito-Lay) for a while. Well, one day I was coming out of Cleveland headed home and decided to stop in a diner and get a cup of coffee. I got into a conversation with another driver and he asked me where I hailed from. When I told him my home was in Ontonagon, he straightened up and got real serious and said, "Did you ever do the Military Hill?" I said yes and told him my story. He said, "I made one run through there and I'll quit before I ever take another." He was pulling about twenty tons of freight and when he neared the Hill, he saw the signs but ignored them, said he was doing about forty miles an hour when he broke over the top. Of course, then it was too late to slow down. He said it was like being on a roller coaster when you get to the top of the first hill and look straight down. The longer he talked, the more fired up he got. He said, "I've driven every state in this country, and I've never seen anything like that hill and I'll never know how I came out of it alive. How did they allow something like that to be built in the first place?"

I then told him my story. One morning, an old neighbor of ours knocked on our door and wanted to talk to our dad. It seems the co-op store in town ran short of cattle feed and asked Rigu if he would be interested in making a few bucks with his truck. Of course he agreed and the manager said he needed about 125 bags (about 6 tons) of feed brought in from Bruce's Crossing Store. He said he'd pay two dollars a ton. Rigu, of course, jumped at the chance to make that kind of easy money. Where could you get twelve dollars in one day with so little work involved?

Well, it turned out his truck (a '37 Ford) had two bad tires and he was worried they may not be able to take that much weight. He asked if we would haul the feed and he'd give us eight dollars and help us load and unload the truck.

24

There wasn't even a second thought. Dad said sure, he'd be glad to make the trip. The only trouble was he had a serious back problem and couldn't do any of the work nor even ride in the truck. He said I could go with Rigu, who questioned my ability to handle the Military Hill. Dad said, "He's a better driver than either one of us." So off we went.

On the way out we looked over the situation and agreed it was in good shape. There were some ruts and rough spots, but overall it didn't seem too bad. There hadn't been any rain for awhile so at least it wouldn't be slippery (when the red clay gets rained on it's like an ice rink.) We got loaded and headed back. It was a heavy load: six tons on a one ton chassis ('35 Chevy), but we were sure we had enough horses to get up the Military.

At the top of the hill I stopped and we checked the load and crossed our fingers. When you go down a long hill, even though you have brakes, you let the engine do as much braking as you can. You start down in a low gear until the weight of the load pushes you faster. Well then the engine begins to rev up in RPMs so you shift to a higher gear. It'll blow the motor to bits if it winds up too high. About a third of the way down I had to up-shift to second gear and we were gaining speed fast. All at once the engine slowed to an idle and I immediately knew we had lost our drive train and were free-wheeling down the Military. (We later found the clutch disk had come apart, disconnecting the engine from the transmission.)

It's unbelievable how fast the momentum picked up. We were in a free fall. I even considered telling Rigu to jump out and I would too, and let it go, but I knew the lock on his door didn't work, so he couldn't open it. The truck had mechanical brakes and I was standing on the pedal. It was about as good as putting my foot out and dragging it on the ground. Now we were, like the country music song goes, "A rocket sled on rails." I figured if we got to the bottom and could make the sharp curve at the bridge we'd be home free. It seemed like hours but was only seconds, I guess, when the turn came up. I hugged the left side of the road as far as I could, and when I got into the turn I made it as wide as I could. As we rounded the curve, the front wheels were turned and were throwing gravel under the fenders. It sounded like a Jack Hammer. We crashed through the bridge in one piece and I'm sure that old Chevy broke the all-time speed record on that hill. Chuck Yeager broke the space-flight record, but I distinctly heard what I thought was a sonic boom!

We finally coasted to a stop. I looked at Rigu and he had both hands wrapped around the hand brake. It never worked since we owned the truck. His knuckles were white. He was gnashing his teeth and his eyes were like two big saucers. He was shaking like a dog passing peach seeds. It took a couple minutes before either of us spoke. Just then, a car came by and the driver called out and asked if we were in trouble. I said, "No. We're just going to try a little fly fishing long as we're here." He said okay and left.

They rebuilt the Military Hill and made a new bridge some years ago. It's a nice modern-day crossing. There is, however, one more bridge and hill like the Military crossing the Ontonagon about three miles west of Rockland on the way to Victoria. It isn't quite as bad, but still very steep and winding and dangerous during snow or rainy seasons. Also, with the modern-day vehicles with powerful engines and power brakes, it doesn't even cross your mind that it might be dangerous. However, if you're in a 1925 Chevy or Model-T Ford, I'm sure your passenger might want to get out and walk and catch you on the other side and not tempt fate. At least with horses and wagons they never thought much about safety on the Hill.

School Days

When I became of age to begin school it was only a couple of more years before we were taking the bus to town. We had a one room school on Firesteel Road just a short way from our house and I spent my first two years there. I was one of only twelve kids and it went from kindergarten to the eighth grade. The first day they discovered I would be the only one in kindergarten and there was only one in 1st grade so they decided we'd both be first graders. We were, of course, all in one room. It was nice, clean, with a big pot bellied stove in the middle of the room. Teacher would have the older boys stoke the fire during the day until one day Uhro filled it with wood and also threw a handful of .22 caliber ammo in at the same time. Well, in a few minutes all hell broke loose. It sounded like a pop corn popper but 100 times louder. She asked him what he did and he said there was a woodpecker in one of the logs!

She was a good teacher, though. She had just taken the job and was from out of state. All the students were Finn and they all talked better Finn than English. One day she said this would be a good time to learn a second language, and perhaps every day you kids could teach me a few new words so by the end of the year I could communicate with your parents, most of whom could speak no English. Boy! Did they pick up on that one! About a month later she saw my mother and said how well she was learning the language. Ma asked her what words she had learned and she began to talk. Ma said, "For goodness sakes don't say any of those words to anyone." They had taught her all the swear words in the Finnish vocabulary.

The next year that I attended they had a new teacher. She was very nice but she had one peculiarity: she would faint without reason. She'd pass out and in a few minutes she'd be all right and be normal again. One day the older boys hatched a plan for the following morning. It was wintertime. After the Pledge of Allegiance everyone sat at their desks. Emil Garstunen was absent, she thought. In about a half hour there was someone really pounding on the front door. She was kind of leery but anyway went to see who it was. Emil had on his grandpa's big bear skin coat and fur hat. When she opened the door he lunged at her and said "Boo!" Needless to say she went immediately into La La Land. All the kids jumped up and roared. Laurence Taurivaara ran up and pulled her skirt up to her neck and said, "I always wanted to see the rest of her."

On another occasion, the kids were all at their desks doing their lessons and Laurence Leiviska had found a blasting cap on their farm. When they cleared the land they used dynamite to blast out the stumps, and for that they needed the caps to set off the charge. Well, he took out his jack knife and started picking at the cap when it exploded and blew off all his fingers on his right hand except his pinky.

Every boy in the county carried a knife: it was standard equipment. The best Christmas present I ever got was a pair of high top leather boots with a pouch on the right one and a knife inside. I think I wore them to bed for about two weeks.

One thing about the school: the teacher would live in town and would drive out every day. The board hired my mother to go out every morning and shovel out a parking spot for her car and make the fire so it would be warm when class started. Sometimes there would be a five foot drift to clear and often they brought in green wood and it would be difficult to get burning. She would at times spend a few hours cleaning the room and doing everything to get the class started on time. One of the neighbor women was jealous of ma for making money on the side and reported her to the county authorities. A man came out and said they were going to cut off our relief (welfare) because she was making extra money. The relief was $12 a month and she was paid $3 a month for the school job. She pleaded with him to keep the $12 and she quit the side job. The woman who reported her went to the board and wanted the job but didn't get it.

Sometimes one of the kids would bring his gun to school, usually a .22, and at lunch time or after school we would practice our shooting skills. Every road sign for two miles around was like a sieve, there were so many bullet holes in them. Another target was the glass insulators on the electric poles. As soon as they were replaced they were blasted again.

All of the children who attended the school lived within about three miles and walked through the snow taking turns breaking the trail. They all carried their lunch in five pound empty lard pails. We were fortunate living so close and could go home for lunch and have a hot meal. Most of the boys only went about 6 grades and quit to work either on the farm or in the saw mills or lumber camps. A lot of the girls went on to graduate but again quite a few opted to work at home.

There was a trap door in the ceiling of the classroom and sometimes in the summer months the teacher would have her lunch outside with some of the kids. The boys would go up into the attic and play in the darkness. One day Tubby was cavorting around with the older boys (he was about seven or eight) in the dark and apparently fell asleep. The other kids came down and closed the trap door, the classes started and when he woke up he realized what had happened but was afraid to make noise or come down because we had all been warned not to go up there. The teacher thought he had run home and thought no more about it. Well, about three o'clock Tub had to go to the bathroom and now what should he do? If he came out he would be punished. He decided to just go on the attic floor. It so happened he went right over the teacher's desk and as she was getting everyone's attention suddenly something started to drip over her head and shoulders. It wasn't raining and there was no other way water could be coming down. She opened the trap door and whacked poor Tub a couple of good licks to the amusement of everybody.

In the winter the teacher parked her '31 Chevy in the little parking area ma had shoveled out and hurried into the class room because it was always 10 or 20 below zero. As soon as she closed the door and just before classes began some of the older boys would pack a bunch of snow around the back wheels and throw four or five pails of water on it. By three or four in the afternoon she had huge blocks of ice on each wheel. Imagine a 21 year old girl in that weather trying to get her car out (even if she did get the engine started).

They built a brand new elementary school in town a few years later and we rode to school in a brand new '35 Chevy bus. That first ride was like going to heaven and the school was unbelievable. We wondered if we should take our boots off to go to class. Our moms told us all to be sure to clean all the barn stuff off them so we wouldn't stink

Waiting for the bus

the room up. Now we were all in our own grade, even though some only had a half dozen or so in each grade. The little city of Rockland close by would sometimes have two or three kids in the graduation class. Now, of course, they're bussed in from fifteen or twenty miles away.

The Dance Hall

First, I'd like to explain that when all the homesteaders got settled in on their land in our area, nobody had much money so they all got together and pooled their resources and formed a co-op so it would allow them to buy things that would have been impossible for one family to afford. They had several investments – most importantly they had shares in a general store in Ontonagon. Later on they opened about four or five more in Mass City, Wasas Siding, one in northern Wisconsin, and I think one or two more. They could charge their goods and if for some reason someone didn't pay, the co-op would take it out of their shares in the company.

Also they invested in a threshing machine and tractor and at harvest time would go from one farm to another until all had their grain safely in silos. I think they grew mostly oats and barley for feed – an investment like that wouldn't possibly be affordable by one farmer. After all the investors' grain was in the silo they could do others and make enough to pay for the operation – there wasn't any labor cost because everyone in the co-op worked for the group without pay. The Mass Co-op Stores, as it was known, must have lasted at least seventy five years as far as I know. My family held shares in it for most of the time.

They had (I think) forty acres right next to my grandfather's property where they built the one-room school which was where I was enrolled. There was about twelve or fifteen acres of clearing where the school stood and at the opposite end they all got together, sawed the lumber and erected a huge dance hall. It was about thirty feet by sixty, and was well made. There was a big stage at one end and a big kitchen in front. On dance nights, the women would prepare coffee, Finnish Nissu and Pulla – a kind of coffee cake – very delicious. During the dance, people could go and have refreshments. The hall had a beautiful hardwood floor upon which they would throw cornmeal to make it slippery. There were benches the length of the walls where people would sit and wait to dance. Everyone was in their Sunday best and it was quite spectacular when the polka and schottische were playing and about fifty or sixty people were spinning around the floor.

There was a big front porch at the entrance – about twelve feet square and all the young single men would stand out there and watch the proceedings. Most were too bashful to go in and ask a girl for a dance. Many had beer or liquor in their cars and every half hour or so they'd sneak out and take a hit. Well, along about ten or eleven o'clock the front porch came alive – shouting and shoving each other around, and inevitably there were fist fights to see who was the better fighter.

We lived only about 100 yards from the hall, so even when I was twelve or thirteen we would go to see the action. Behind the stage was a trap door leading to the outside. We would sneak in there to avoid paying the ten or fifteen cents cover charge – we never had any money. The people in charge probably knew we didn't pay but looked the other way.

All my buddies would mingle with the people but when I got in I went on the stage and sat there all night just watching the accordion player. They also had a man playing

the piano keeping time. I stayed out of sight behind the
curtain so no one ever knew I was there except
the accordion man. I'd sit there all night long until they

Still playing the accordion

finished. I guess that's why I always wanted an accordion but
never had one until I grew up. I still have one now and still
play all those old songs I heard on the stage of the Firesteel
Dance Hall.

There were so many people running around in the dark
during the dance. The outhouses were about 100 feet away

and people would lose things in the dark. Early the next morning we'd go and search the grounds and always find things, articles of clothing, tobacco cans, pipes, and often when the men would wrestle and fight, their wallets and loose change would fall out of their pockets and we'd hit the mother lode. One morning my sister went over about daylight to see what she could find and found seven silver dollars – one half month pay for our family. I didn't smoke yet then, but some of the older kids did and they would pick up king size cigarette butts. Everybody rolled their own so now they had real smokes for a while. I didn't know where the term started, but if you bought cigarettes in a package, they were called tailor-mades. You never asked for a pack of cigarettes in a store, you said, "Give me some tailor-mades."

It was fun to watch when the night life was ending. There were cars on both sides of the gravel road for about a quarter mile in each direction. The young guys now were ready to party after sniffing the cork all evening, and, as the girls walked by in the dark, they would yell and scream as the men would try to talk to them. All the old men were out cranking their Model Ts in the mud with their Sunday best on – having to wear it to church in the morning. I learned a lot of choice words also. Eventually they all left, there would be a few whose Maxwells or Stars wouldn't start and would have to be pushed or towed.

The Bag Ladies

During the Great Depression years times were hard – there wasn't any money except for absolute essentials. As I remember, the relief, as we called it, paid my dad about $12 a month. Everything had to be grown in the garden and apple and plum orchards, etc. Clothing was hand-made or hand-me-downs. No automobiles, farming was mostly done by hand. Hay was mowed with scythes, racked up and stacked by hand. Meat was mainly from the woods or river and some farmers who had cattle and hogs usually helped those who didn't have any. I remember our mother telling of writing her sister in Detroit a letter but waited two weeks to mail it because she only had 2¢ and needed another penny for a stamp. Fortunately she happened to locate one while rummaging around in an old trunk in back of the farm.

We had a fairly well off neighbor who was a real miser. They had a big farm and thumbed their noses at the "have-nots". I think I was about 11 years old when one morning just before day break he came pounding on our front door. He wanted me to come help with the haying and of course I was eager to go – and earn some money. They had a 1924 Overland car that had the body removed (we called them Bugs) and I pulled a mower with it. Well it was about 5 A.M. that I started and drove until noon. They did give me a good lunch and a water bottle to keep with me, and I drove until about 9 P.M., just about dark. When I finished he said he had things to do so I'd have to walk home. I was so tired that I laid down along the road before I got home. As I was preparing to leave he said, "Wait, I'll pay you for your work." He handed me a nickel. Talk about starvation wages!

The saying was that nickels looked like wagon wheels – he had that in mind I guess.

It's hard for anyone today to imagine that kind of life, but it's like being in the service; everybody is in the same boat. We didn't go around wringing our hands and gnashing our teeth. In fact, when we had enough to eat and keep warm we were reasonably happy. It was no use complaining, it wouldn't make it better.

We used to make periodic trips to the town dump to look for treasures. Dad would go sometime but it was usually our mom. It was a five mile walk so if they found anything worthwhile it would be difficult to carry home. She always took a big gunny sack used for cattle feed and would try to fill it up, then drag it home. All sorts of goodies came from there – broken wagons, scooters, anything my dad could repair and he could do anything. Lots of old jelly glasses (our drinking glasses), all sorts of jars, all used for canning, even old broken chairs. Anything that could be carried home.

One day we were on top of the pile and a man came over, very irate, and said, "This is my pile. If you want to dig, go over to the other side!" Another time mom and Elma Torp were both on their way home dragging their sacks. Elma was so slow mom went on ahead. A few hours later Elma came over to our house and told mom, "Boy was I lucky! Some people came along and gave me a ride." Of course mom was glad for her and told her so. Elma replied, "When I got in the car we started driving and the man said, 'Look there's another lady with a sack. Do you know her?" She said "No I don't know who it is so you don't need to pick her up." Mom asked why she told him that. Elma said that she "didn't think there was enough room in the car for both of us with our bags."

Toward the end of the depression they started to hand out some food, just as they do today. There was cheese, fruit, canned meat, vegetables, etc. which helped many people. Our small town had a few officials who handed out this government surplus and they tried to impress upon all the people how lucky they were to have these good Samaritans helping the poor, when in fact they didn't have a hand in it except to hand the food out at the rail yard. One person owned the only department store in town and was quite affluent. When people went to him to pick up the 25 lbs. bags of flour he said it would cost 50¢. My dad said the bags had a large government stamp on them that said NOT TO BE SOLD. He just said to pay up or get the hell out of here so I can take care of someone else. Needless to say our monthly flour allotment was zero that time.

The relief check was used mostly for coffee, sugar, salt and things we couldn't grow ourselves. Things were very cheap but the money just wasn't there. Eggs were 6¢ a dozen, milk was 3¢ a quart, store bread just 5¢ a loaf, etc., etc. You could buy a bag of Bull Durham cigarette tobacco that would make about 50 cigarettes when you rolled your own for 5¢. Gasoline was at one time 5 gallons for 88¢.

I had my first car when I was about 12; it was a 1929 Whippet. I used to go to our neighbors to buy gas: they had a lot of farm machinery and kept barrels of gas all the time. He used to sell me a quart for 5¢, so every time I had a nickel I could drive some. If I had a dime I could go to the river and go swimming.

At about the same time dad built a small barn so we could get a cow; then we'd have our own milk and butter. Well, after the barn was done there was a problem. There was no money for a cow. After a lot of negotiations mom's sister Edna came up with a plan. She would give us a good cow for our leather living room couch. Now we had milk and there was so much more than we could use that we got a pig. Every spring we'd get one and butcher it in the fall. So now we even had ham, pork chops, head cheese, etc. and things were definitely on the upside.

I was still a little young to get a real job but the paper mill in town started taking pulp wood so being we had a lot of Aspen on our property it seemed like a good supplement to our relief check. Dad had a real problem with his back and just couldn't do heavy work. Mom had the idea that she and I could cut pulp. Neither of us knew anything at that time about cutting trees down. We'd saw a little then we'd take turns chopping and when it was ready to fall we had no way of knowing which way it was going to fall. We'd throw down our tools and run and then come back and start sawing it up. It was heavy, heavy work. Green Poplar in 5' sticks 6" in diameter had to be 75 lbs. at least.

Everything we did was the hard way. The saw and axes we had were so dull it would take hours to cut just a few sticks. We'd cut the tree up, carry them out and pile them by the road. Later we'd hand load them on the truck, drive to the mill, unload by hand and pile it up in the milk yard. A cord was a pile 4' high and 8' long. For all that we were paid $4 and we paid the trucker $1 a cord so our total profit from days and days of hard work was $3 – not very lucrative to say the least.

40

At one time some organization was handing out articles of clothing. I remember dad getting a heavy leather mackinaw which he wore for many years. I walked into town with mom and dad to get it and we just couldn't believe our good fortune. There were a couple of women there to help try on the clothes. An old man named Lehto Antti lived down the road from us in an old shack. He was about 5' 2". Real short. Well, when we walked in a woman was fitting him for a pair of pants. The pair she held in front of him came over his neck; his little bald head was the only thing showing and he was yelling," I TANK YOU, I TANK YOU."

In the wintertime I also had a trap line in the woods nearby. Weasels are only taken in winter because the ermine is white only at that time. In the summer they are brown in color and there is no value for their fur. I would get up an hour early so I could make the round on my skis through the woods. It was usually below zero and a lot of snow. If I caught one I would skin it after school and stretch the hide out on a board for a couple of weeks, curing it before sending it in. There were a few companies in Chicago who dealt in furs but I always sent mine to Sears & Roebuck because they seemed to pay a little more than the others.

A large pelt would pay about 15¢, a medium about 8¢ or 10¢ and I even once got 2¢ for a small one. There were a lot of muskrats too, and I trapped them in the summer; a few mink and beaver but not too many. The beaver season was only a couple of weeks and I could never afford a license for them. We had tons of rabbits but only for meat; the hides weren't worth anything.

Also I hunted deer every season. I could never afford a license for deer either, but there was only one game warden for our county and not much chance of getting caught. Even if we were arrested the penalty was that you would lose your right to hunt for three years. I never bought a license anyway so who cares!

Winter Travel

In the years of the Great Depression, when I was born (1928), hardly anyone owned an automobile. If they did, it was probably parked in a field because there wasn't any money for gas, let alone license plates, although usually nobody bothered to buy plates until much later, maybe the late 30's.

Consequently, walking was the main form of transportation. Ma and dad thought nothing of walking us all to the neighbors 6 or 7 miles away for a visit and coming home at night feeling our way on a muddy road.

About 1934 dad bought a '27 Chevy and boy we thought we were rich. He taught me to drive it and at age eight I was handling it just fine through the snow or mud. It didn't have a heater and we'd all put on heavy coats, boots, etc. and then blankets as well. The windows would have a half inch of frost and dad would have a small hole about 6" square to look through. Also he would have a little cloth bag with salt in it, and he'd keep rubbing it over the hole and it would be all blurry but there usually wasn't anyone else on the road so he could just watch the high snow banks and stay between them.

We kids would sit in the back seat and write or draw pictures on the frosty glass. If you wanted to erase the writing you'd just wait a few minutes and at minus 30° it would freeze over and you'd have a new surface.

I still wonder how those old cars would start on a cold morning.

When I started working – I was 14 – I had a Model A Ford and it wouldn't be any use even trying the starter. I'd take the hand crank out of the car and I'd have to stand on it to turn the engine over a dozen or so times. The oil was just like heavy grease. Many times we'd pile some cedar sticks under the engine and throw some gas on them and light them to warm the oil before it would fire up.

We didn't have permanent type anti-freeze and some people used kerosene in the radiator. I used alcohol but it would boil over if I kept the bear skin over the radiator too long. There wasn't a temp gauge so I'd stop after a few miles and throw the skin in the back seat. Also, every time I'd buy gas I'd put about a pint of alcohol in the tank because there were always frozen carburetors and gas lines.

My Uncle Ed drove a logging truck (I think it was a '38 Ford) and he kept it at home every night. When I'd wait for the school bus I'd go and watch him start it up. After he built the fire and got the engine started he had to build another one under the rear axle housing or he couldn't move. He had a '36 International at home one time and tried to take off before he warmed up the rear end and the drive shaft broke in two.

Another no-no was never have it parked in gear, always in neutral because when you cranked it, if it wasn't in neutral, you couldn't get it out of gear until the 90# transmission oil warmed up or you would break the shift lever right off.

I think the reason was the lubricants weren't anything like today and the steel wasn't as good either. One of our neighbors had a 29' Chevy sedan and he broke so many rear axles he would buy two at a time so he'd always have a spare.

44

Some of the regular equipment you would need to carry at all times were –shovel and axe, antifreeze, can of

Digging out the stake truck

gas and some cedar in case you got stranded and had to build a fire, tow chain, tire chains, flashlight or lantern, and dry mitts.

I had to drive 23 miles to the woods and most of it was on logging roads. There were a lot of other workers but I drove the snow plow and had to leave home about 2:30 A.M. so I'd have the road open for the others. That meant I was the first one on the road and if we had a storm it was a long hard trip. Sometimes I wouldn't get there until 8 and everyone was upset because the road wasn't plowed.

One of the lumberjacks one morning said, "Ed don't put your tongue on the pump handle this morning 'cause it's 38° below zero!

Everyone heard and talked about 4 wheel drive vehicles but we had never seen one and wondered about how much of an improvement it would be.

Well, when the war started in 1941 there was a doctor in town that got hold of someone with influence and said he had to have one of those 4 wheel drive Jeeps. Lo and behold a few weeks later they delivered one with canvas roof, side curtains, and the whole 9 yards. He was so proud he parked it in front of his office and the whole town gathered around and looked it over. He came out and proclaimed how it was almost impossible to get stuck with the new 4 wheel drive. Well that was all he had to say when a bunch of the young blades standing there said, "You'd better prove it".

He said follow me down to the four corners and I'll show you. I guess there were 12 or 14 cars trailing him and when he stopped there he said, "I'll make a lap around this 40 acre field and show you what I can do." Everybody laughed and said, "All right, let's see!"

46

He got in and backed up for a flying start. When he got over the snow bank he was going around 25 miles an hour, the engine in the Jeep was screaming. He did go about 150 yards when he stopped and the jeep slowly settled and almost disappeared. He tried to move but even with chains on all 4 wheels it never moved again.

He crawled out and said, "Would someone please go down the road and ask Bruno Darrow to bring his team of horses?" A big cheer went up from the crowd and he sheepishly said, "I didn't think it was that deep or I would have made it."

One more story about the snow and cold. We'd have storms that today are unbelievable. My dad and I went to the middle of the road in front of our house after an April storm and put a pole down through the snow and it measured exactly 12 feet. We had already gotten electricity and the wires were lying right on top of the snow.

The county Road Commission opened the road but it took over a week. They had a huge HOLT crawler-tractor (it was the forerunner of Caterpillar) which had an auger type blower in front. They called it a Sno-Go. It would slice right through the banks but it was slow.

When the driver got through he'd shut it off right where he stopped and the next morning when he'd come to start it up (it was diesel) he would take a 3 gallon can of gasoline and pour it all over the engine and light a match to it. It was the only way it would start. The fuel oil would be almost congealed and that was the only solution.

When I worked in the woods they let the diesel tractors run all night or they'd never start in the morning. If you were to go to town on a Saturday morning you would see a few farmers pulling their cars with a horse to get it started. No heated garages here!

Some people even carried a pair of skis in the car in case they got stranded. It was much easier than trying to walk.

In those days in the area we were in, horses and sleighs were a lot better alternative because even if the plow came by, if it was stormy, inside of an hour the road was impassable.

I often think what a valuable asset a come-a-long would have been with about 150 feet of one quarter inch cable. It sure would have saved a lot of pushing and shoving. Today one can be purchased for about $15 and how valuable it would have been.

The Camp

I was prepared to write of some camp life I had experienced in my younger years as a lumberjack, and the more I thought about it I began to realize I probably worked in the last, or at least one of the last big-time logging operations in that part of the country. It was called Michigan Slims Camp; he ran the operation although most of the timber taken was from Henry Ford's land. Ford owned large tracts of timber in northern Michigan ever since he began building automobiles. The wood was used for wheels and bodies on the old Fords; the first all-steel cars didn't emerge until the late '30's so he had a big demand for wood. Also, there were several paper mills, and numerous saw mills providing lumber for the building boom around that time.

Many people have never heard or known what a lumber camp operation is like except that the final result is a load of logs being made into paper or lumber. I'll try to create an image of the workings and the people who make up such a large operation and some of the characters and stories I'd witnessed and the people I've worked with. Within three or four years after I moved away the timber ran out and the camps were shut down, never again to re-open. The big pine trees were taken in the mid and late 1800s and after twenty-five or thirty years the Hemlock, Spruce, and hardwood matured and the big loggers were back in business. The first pine operations were all moved by railroads, which crisscrossed the entire state. There weren't many roads in the area and the ones that were there were a sea of mud all summer as soon as the snow was gone. Also in the early 1900s there weren't any trucks capable of hauling thirty-five-ton loads and horses couldn't handle any more than a couple of logs at a time – hence the railroads.

About the time the forests re-developed and the operations were mechanized, tractors and trucks were used more and more. It was expensive and difficult to build railroads, and after a few months they would have to move to another location and build new tracks through swamps, across rivers, etc. With the new powerful bull dozers and tractors it was much cheaper and faster as they were mobile. When a certain area was cleared they simply moved the camp to another spot and kept right on going. The big "dozers" could make nearly a mile of new road a day right through the standing timber and the new trucks in the late '30s and '40s had powerful engines and yet were relatively light and could easily handle the improved roads.

That phase of Michigan U.P. logging ended for all practical purposes by 1950; again thirty or forty years later they are now harvesting hardwood and a lot of aspen so the cycle is renewed. They now have machines which one man can operate which will cut and pile 100 cords a day, and clear-cutting machines that grind the wood into chips which are blown into covered trailers right on the spot. In the paper mills the wood was always ground up into chips to be processed so now it's done right in the field.

I am now 78 years old so there are not too many people left that had the hands-on experience of life in the world of the Lumber Jack. I'll try to form a mental image and show what life was like and the life-long impressions I've kept in back of my mind. I'll try to remember and write as accurately as I can.

Michigan Slims Camp

He was a huge powerful hulk of a man. He always reminded me of stories of Paul Bunyan. At age fifteen I had never been near anyone who caught my attention more. He walked with a scaler's rule in his hand (it was used to measure the board feet in a log) and he used it like a cane and to emphasize a point or show where he wanted the road built or which trees to cut down. His voice boomed and everyone knew when he was around. He would fire a man without hesitation if he got in an argument or a difference of opinion – he was Michigan Slim – the boss. I think it might have been because of my age and my shyness he always liked me and except for a couple times treated me respectfully. He would say, "Eddie, I'm going to make you into the best damn lumberjack they've ever seen around here." But I always worked hard and when I drove the snow plow one winter I'd work eighteen and even twenty-four hours during storms.

Slim wouldn't even give you much praise but he'd say, "I'll give you a little extra this week." He knew I worked hard – in that business there are no easy jobs, so we got along great.

The camp I was at was about twenty-five miles from home and we all had cars (mine was a '29 Ford) and six of us would take turns driving so it wasn't a big expense for anyone. Also in the winter when we left home the county roads weren't plowed yet at 4:30 A.M., so with six men we could lift the cars out of the drifts if we had to. We carried three or four snow shovels in each car, and there were countless others going to work at the same time, so even with a big storm we all made it.

The camp itself housed about 200 men who stayed there all winter – it was really like a small town; everything they needed was provided. The Bull Cook (chore boy) took care of the stoves all night and of course during the day when it was cold. He had a 55-gallon oil drum made into a heater at each end of each bunk house which took four-foot blocks of wood. They had pipes inside the barrels that connected to another barrel standing upright full of water and stayed very hot all the time. Next to that were a few sinks so men could wash up when they got in.

The bunk beds lined both sides of the room with about a ten foot aisle. The jacks would have all their belongings in gunny sacks tied to their bunk. Needless to say there was a lot of thieving going on and many arguments. The lights were turned off at nine P.M. and it was absolutely quiet for the rest of the night. There was a small four-cylinder engine turning a generator so the twelve-volt system was like regular lighting. After it was turned off, lanterns were used if needed.

There was a huge sauna that could hold twenty five or so at one time which was heated three times a week. An outhouse stood about fifty yards away with lanterns lit along the way all night long. Slims Camp was built on the bank of the Big Sleepy River in Houghton County, Michigan, and the cook shack was right on the edge of the hill. About forty feet down the side hill was a natural spring (artesian well) with clean, cold water bubbling out 24-7 that took care of all fresh water needs for the whole place.

The cook shack was just a few steps from the bunk houses and our cook (Joe) was the best I've ever seen. I've eaten in dozens of restaurants, but none I have seen that could compare with his operation. Everything of course was made from scratch. It was unbelievable to see the meals he had prepared. Any kind of meat or vegetable you could name was to be seen at some time or other. They had tables (like picnic tables) and with 100 men at a time eating, the food kept on coming as fast as it was eaten. Also there was a large table near the door that had coffee and tea, three or four kinds of pie, cookies, sweet rolls, fruit, lunch meat and bread that was available in the morning and evening for snacks. In the morning the jacks would come in and pack their own lunch boxes because they would be gone all day. During the war everything was rationed and no one could buy much coffee, sugar, meat, and things like that. While I was there he had me drive to town a couple times a week to get groceries, or a load of meat. There was a meat house with sides of beef, pork, hams, spare ribs, and about any kind of lunch meat you could want. It looked like a butcher's shop. On other days I'd get a load of ice and pack it in saw dust in the ice house. Other times I'd get a few tons of coal for the tractor sheds.

The lumber business was exempt from rationing because it was vital to the war effort so whatever was needed was available.

There were a couple of big horse barns. During my stay they had about ten teams, besides using the tractor, for skidding and cross hauling when loading the logs on trucks. The teamsters all took care of their own team and made sure they were watered and fed every day. It was a dangerous job and I saw many accidents involving the horses which I'll go into later.

The tractor sheds were heated at night; they were all diesel engines and at 25 to 35 below zero they would never start in the morning. Otherwise, I think Slim had about four TD9 International Cats and a large TD14 Bulldozer when I was there. I drove them all at one time or another, but mostly I drove the log trucks and snow plow.

The next part of the operation was the one I always regretted not asking for – the blacksmith shop. Our guy was Harry and he was an absolute artist in his trade. His forge was going by 6:30 A.M. He made everything in hardware, from horseshoes and tongs to axe handles. He even would make bolts and nuts and all the steel work for the jammers (which he also made). He would install the cables and pulleys and make the hooks (pups) to hold the logs while they were being loaded. All the equipment used was massive. I saw him go to his forge and beat out a wrench to fasten a four-inch-wide bolt to a loader because they didn't have one that large. A steel truck came in every few months and brought cable, pipe, I-beams, angle iron, chains, square and rod steel, and whatever else he needed. When you are working with logs and lumber weighing many tons, there are always breakdowns – chains, cables, wood, and metal failures – so the blacksmith is the most important person you need to rely on to keep things going. From harness parts to shoes and eveners, even the horse equipment needs repairs from time to time.

Also there were a couple of pumps for gasoline and fuel oil for the tractors, and the tractor came out every couple weeks or so to fill the tanks. In the general area of our camp there was another logger a few miles away and between the two camps there must have been about thirty-five trucks. Slim had probably twelve of his own and there were quite a few private owners who hauled from our camp. We had perhaps twenty-four miles of our own roads before getting to the main road, so the truck traffic was always very heavy on the narrow roads. I would say in the winter time you would see an over-turned load at least once a week, especially if the weather warmed and the icy roads were really slippery. The one-and-a-half ton trucks would carry huge loads for their size, usually about 3,000 or more feet per load, weighing roughly 25 tons or more.

The Operation

Now that we know a little about the camp operation, I'll start to try to explain some of the procedures in this lumber business. First of all, they used what was called selective logging; by that I mean the trees to be cut were all marked, not like today where they go in and clear cut and leave nothing. Selective logging is an ongoing operation. Every forty or fifty years you have a new crop and you leave all the young trees to grow for later harvest. As you cut the ones that are full-grown, the sunlight can come in and the land is thinned out to really nourish the next crop.

They used what was called a timber advisor who went ahead and marked the trees to be harvested on probably sixty or eighty acres. Next would be the boss who'd go and blaze the trees where he wanted the road to be built. He would try to avoid swamps and places where bridges would be needed to make it as easy as possible for the dozer to build the road. Dad's brother ran the bulldozer and he was an expert. He could make a finished road with ditches and culverts over three quarters of a mile in a day if the ground was fairly level and not real wet. It is remarkable considering the size of the trees. They could be four feet or more in diameter and he would first go around and break the roots as deep as possible, then push the tree down, and then push it to the side of the road. Slim brought some men in from the government who wanted to check on his operation. Well, they stayed and watched him build that road for two hours. The leader of the group kept saying, "I don't believe what I'm seeing." They were amazed what that machine was doing. Somewhere in Washington is a report and I'm sure it raised some eyebrows about how difficult that machine was to operate and how vital it could be with a good operator. Also, it was very dangerous. I've seen times where he would approach a huge Hemlock and just touch the dozer blade to it to bring it down when a large dead branch six or eight inches in diameter would come crashing 75-feet down right on the machine. There wasn't time to shift into reverse to avoid it, so the operator would just leap off his seat and run and hope he could get away in time. Another unseen danger which he was unable to avoid was what we called "spring poles." When you drive the machine through the woods you naturally run over a lot of brush and saplings. Well, when you do that many times a small tree will be bent right down to the ground and it might break off. When that happens it's like a rubber band and it snaps back like a shot. If it comes in the direction of the driver it could kill him. I saw men lose their arms, another lost three fingers, and a third one got hit in the groin and had to be castrated.

One other thing that really plagued everyone was the flies and mosquitoes during the summer and fall. It's unbelievable how vicious they can be. We would go to the diesel fuel pump and fill a can with fuel oil every morning around 9 A.M. When the auger came out we would take a rag, dip it in fuel oil, and wash our hands and face. It was the only way you could withstand the rush of the hoard.

The operator could never be alone in the woods. He had to have an assistant (swamper) at all times just for that reason. His job was to pick up small brush and wood or rocks left on the road when it was being finished. He also had to grease the rollers on the dozer tracks twice a day and before it was parked he needed to get all the chunks of mud from underneath so it didn't freeze overnight. The old man at our camp was John; he'd had that job for several years and when they drove to the tractor barn at night he'd be riding on the blade holding onto the hydraulic hoses. I used to tease John by saying, "You're getting bow-legged from riding that machine." He'd laugh and tell me in Finn, "Mene Helinettun" (Go to Hell).

Sawyers

The next phase after the roads and skidways were done was the cutting of the timber. About every half- mile on the road, there would be an area of about one-half acre where the trees were brought and lined up to be loaded on the trucks. There were two-man crews. They used two-man crosscut saws (chainsaws didn't come until the mid-1940s) and they would cut a notch on the side facing where they wanted it to fall. Then they'd cut the opposite side about three quarters of the way through. They made wedges and would drive a wedge in the crack made by the saw so it wouldn't bind from the weight of the huge tree. They also used kerosene on the saw to make it slippery. Spruce and Hemlock, especially, have a lot of gum that chokes up the saw otherwise. When the tree slowly began to fall they would drop the saw and run. Sometimes a falling tree will go into what we called a "Barber Chair," meaning that if it happened to fall onto another standing tree with its speed and force it could bend the other tree down. Well, when that happens the other tree will be the same as a spring pole and snap back up, sending the falling tree back like a rocket, smashing everything due to its tremendous weight. Many, many jacks lost their lives that way.

One evening when all the men came in for supper and sat down, Slim sat at the head of the table and asked at once, "Where's Gus Pennala?" His seat was empty – no one remembered him coming in. Slim jumped up and said, "Son of a bitch. He was sawing alone today." Slim took a few men and they got in his pickup and tore out of the camp to where Gus was working. When they arrived, they found Gus lying on the ground, a giant Hemlock had buried him up to his waist – a Barber Chair had gotten him before he could get away. He was conscious, and when they ran up to him he said, "Please take the axe and hit it into my head." He had lain under that tree since noon. Slim told Fred to take his pickup and go for an ambulance while the others cut the tree in two and pulled Gus out. Gus only lost one leg, fortunately, but he screamed the whole time 'til the doctor got there to give him a shot and take him away. When those large trees are felled, they smash a lot of saplings, too, and when the sawyers trim the branches, often they'll be hit by spring poles, especially in winter. The tree falls and is buried in a couple feet of snow so you can't see what's underneath.

The trees were cut into different lengths to utilize all the available wood – usually 12-14-16 foot. If they cut pulp wood it was eight-foot pieces. During their lunch hour, one man would file the saw and the other would sharpen the axes with a file. At the end of the day a scaler would come by after the sawyers left and scale the board feet in every log. He would enter the amount in a ledger and write the figures on the stump for the logs from each tree so the sawyers would know how much money they had made that day. In the '40s in our camp, they made one-and-one-quarter cents per board foot. If the terrain was good and conditions were okay, they made pretty good money for that period.

Skidders

When those huge trees are felled and cut up, there are a lot of brush and limbs all around. So in order for the horses or "Cat" (crawling tractor) to get to the logs you need to have a swamper to go in and clear a path so the tongs can be hooked to the log. The swamper chops away the underbrush, then when the Cat backs up to the log, the swamper places the tongs so it can be pulled to the skidway. When the log begins to move he will get out of the way, because while being pulled and snaked through the woods the log will hang on a tree and swing like a cow's tail and the small spring poles will start really snapping. That is the reason the teamsters job with horses is so dangerous. The load is so heavy the horses will pull really hard and they won't stop if the teamster loses his footing, in which case he'll fall right into the path of the log being pulled. Imagine holding the reins of a running team of horses in snow and fallen brush and trying to stay on your feet over stumps and knells and water holes. I had a buddy whose name was Andrew. He was probably about fifty-five years old and came from Sweden (there were jacks from all over the world at the camp). He was a sawyer and sometimes drove a team, if needed. He was like my Pa – I guess because I was so young, he'd say, "Eddy, boy, ven da camp shut down next spring, und ve com back in da fall, I don't vant to see you no more here. I vas vunce nice boy lak you and come to lumber camp. Now look vat I am – old, broke, no home, notting to live for. You are now young, smart – you end up lak me if you don't get killed first. You'll travel the world lak me, a nobody. Just try to stay live." In the evenings, after supper, he would sit and do wood carvings. I guess that's what inspired me to do it. It was just remarkable the things he'd carve. He'd make teams of horses with all the harnesses, sleighs full of logs, tractors, trucks, busts of some of the other jacks, he even carved one of me in my snowplow and they were all perfect. He offered

60

me some of them and I wouldn't take them because I knew how much work he put into them. I wish I'd taken at least one to remember him. Who knows where that stuff ended up?

The logs were pulled to the skid-way and lined up side-by-side to be loaded on the trucks, which were lined up waiting for their load. It was a continuous operation. The team and tractors worked without stopping to keep things moving. Each skid-way had maybe three or four skidders working full time, depending on the terrain.

There were several rivers and deep ravines to be logged out also. When the sawyers cut the trees on the side of a hill and the horses couldn't get them up the steep incline, there was a big Cat (Caterpillar) with a winch and about 100 feet of cable to pull them up to level ground. I did that for a few weeks, too. I had to drag the cable way down the steep bank, hook the tongs to the log, then follow it up and drag it down again. That was a hell of a job for about three dollars per day. After the tongs were put on the log we'd yell to the operator to pull it up. Sometimes it was far and with the engine running he couldn't hear so you needed to run back up the hill and tell him to start.

One day I asked Bill Ahola (the operator) why he didn't just wait five minutes and start the cable so I wouldn't have to run and make another trip up the hill. He said a couple of years before they had done it that way and an operator started to pull the log and the hooker got his arm caught up somehow in the tongs and yelled but wasn't heard. By the time the log got up the hill he was all in pieces under the log.

In the spring, when the snow was gone and the frost was out of the ground, the roads were impassible with mud holes, so most of the operation nearly came to a halt. The sawyers could keep working if they wanted, so they kept sawing and the skidders pulled the logs to the skid-ways. They had jammers (used to load the trucks) and some were portable, mounted on the backs of trucks with another engine and winch used to make huge deck piles (logs piled up about twenty feet high and lined up alongside the roads). By winter, there were hundreds of logs in decks and as soon as the ground froze and snow came and trucks could haul again, they'd have crews loading those as well as the regular winter operation. By the end of the year everything was humming again. The camp was so far from the nearest town the jacks couldn't get there to hire in, so Slim would go to a few of their favorite bars and tell the owner what kind of help he needed and they would put the jacks in a cab and send them out to camp. When spring came, the lumberjacks would have their whole winter's pay when they got to town. Most would get drunk and broke in a short time and just hang around the bars until fall, when they were glad to get back and have a place to eat and sleep again. Most didn't have a home or friends to go to so that was their entire life – work all winter and bum around all summer. In the earlier days when the farms were homesteaded, the farmers would give them room and board for the summer and they would clear the land and make wood for the winter. They were glad to do it as their money was all gone and they had nowhere else to go.

That was the way most of the farmers' fields were cleared: with the help of the jacks. If you think about it, when you see a big area of 80 or 120 acres, you never give a thought that it was once all wooded. And at the turn of the century, it was all done by hand. Some of the luckier ones had teams of horses but all but a few chopped the trees down, pulled the stumps out by hand, – I'm talking about stumps four to six feet in diameter – digging down four to six feet again to cut the huge roots. Then, if you had dynamite, you'd blow the rest out of the ground, then either cut it up in pieces or, if you knew someone with horses, have them come drag it away. They cut all the trees up for wood for their heaters, but then there were a million branches to pile up and after they dried out a few weeks they were burnt. Once the area was reasonably clean came another big project. If you ever walked in the woods I know you've seen it isn't all level. There are knolls and hills every ten or twenty feet, so now you don't have a bulldozer and you need to level each one with a grub hoe. Picture trying to swing a grub hoe into a ground full of roots and trying to make a level surface. In the county we lived the soil was all heavy red clay, which after it dried out was like Portland cement. Imagine trying to swing a hoe into that.

We only had a small home place but we, too, had to try to clear part of it so we could raise a few crops and grow enough hay to feed a few cows through winter. We had a lumberjack named John Hakala who liked our family and in the spring he would come and live with us all summer to help with anything we needed done. He was a very hard worker and there wasn't any question of pay. My dad was on relief at the time and his total income was sixteen dollars a month. John would say, "I just need to eat and have a place to sleep. If I had money I would go into town and get drunk and spend it right away anyhow. Don't worry, things are going to get better for you when we get this place in shape."

Like most of the other jacks, John would go to camp as soon as they opened in the fall, usually around November or whenever it got cold and we got our first snow so the roads would freeze and the trucks could start hauling again. He stayed in camp all winter and never left until about April when the spring "break up" started.

The men had all their winter wages piled up and were paid off when the camp closed in the spring. Well, the majority of them had no home or anywhere to go so they would go to town and get drunk. All the bar owners were waiting with open arms, of course, so when the jacks came in they'd pour drinks into them until they passed out. They would usually have a couple of rooms in back where they'd drag them and let them sleep it off. When they awoke they'd be hung over and sick so the barkeep would throw a couple of bottles of rot-gut into the room and the cycle was renewed. They had no idea what happened to their money so after about ten days or so they were told to either come up with more money or the drinks were cut off and they would have to leave. If they questioned the bar owner about their money he would just say, "Well, you passed out and another drunk probably rolled you." Now they were sick, hungry, and broke without a place to live all summer. The thought of staying on a farm and clearing land or whatever was just the break they needed to survive until next winter. And of course the homesteaders were more than happy to get experienced woodsmen to help them and were glad to board them all summer. Thus is the life of the lumberjack. Like Andrew told me, "Don' come back this place no more – you will save yer life." Excellent advice.

The Truckers

A person would think that hauling the timber to market would most likely be the safest and easiest part of the entire operation, but it would be an understatement to say it is as soft a job as it appears. The wood is so heavy and the roads so treacherous, a new truck at that time would be completely shot, worn out, battered, and ready for retirement after only three winters. Unbelievably, some of the most common repairs made were to the wheels and springs. The steel wheels would just collapse under the strain, and springs were fitted with three or four extra leafs because they simply couldn't stand the weight of a twenty-five or thirty-ton load. Don't forget, in 1940, 1941, etc., Ford, Chevy, and Dodge only made 1.5-ton capacity vehicles. There were, of course, other large ones like International, but they were so much heavier that the roads wouldn't stand the weight so they were always stuck. Once the lighter trucks got moving, you couldn't stop anywhere except on a good, long, level stretch or you wouldn't have enough power to get rolling again. The company roads were usually only about the width of an average driveway, probably eleven or twelve feet, and about every 100 or so yards they would have a turn-off so the oncoming traffic could pull off to let the loaded trucks proceed. When pulling a load of that size, you needed to think ahead for sometimes three or four miles. You needed to know if there was a long grade or steep hill so you could get your speed to fifty m.p.h. or so. That was the only way you'd get over it as the small trucks just didn't have enough power, otherwise. If you didn't run it, and ran out of power, the driver would just bail out and let the rig run off into the ditches. I have seen many, many, loads turned over and trucks wrecked on steep hills. Another hazard was that if it was slippery in winter, trying to keep that top-heavy, thirty-ton load on the road of ice at fifty m.p.h. was a nerve-wracking experience. When that load starts to slide or fishtail, you don't have a whole lot of control anymore. You always think about hitting a ditch and the full load crashing over your cab. Sometimes, even if your front wheel hits a small drift you'll be pulled right into the bank so you just have to try to keep it on the road.

I had one bad experience while driving. I was on my last load of the day (a real high one), and I was nearing the Firesteel River Hill. I meant to run it. The hill was very steep and there was a narrow bridge to cross. It was really icy and already dark, so I thought that if I didn't make it, or if I met another car on the narrow, slippery road, it could be a disaster. I stopped at the top and decided to put the tire chains on to be sure I wouldn't slide off into the river. I let the engine idle to keep warm and of course left the headlights on while I started putting the chains on the left wheel. Well, a car came along from my front and he, too, had to run the slippery River Hill. I imagine his speed when he came over the hill was about forty m.p.h. Well, as soon as he topped the hill on the narrow road he ran into my bright lights and got blinded and, of course, couldn't see anything. There I was, stooped over in the middle of the road on my knees, and before I could even move he hit me. I think I was probably thrown about 60 feet. I'm not sure if the driver even knew that he ran into me – he never stopped. I got up to see if I was okay and went back to put the irons on. I think because I had so many heavy clothes on I never got a scratch. I must have had four or five layers of shirts, long-johns, sweaters, and a mackinaw, so that probably saved my life.

In the woods, if there was a very steep hill, they would always have a "Cat" to pull the trucks over. Also, early in the fall or spring, if the roads weren't frozen there would be deep mud holes and we would have to be pulled along to get to firm ground.

Another dangerous part of driving was that when you got your load to the mill, a scaler would measure the board feet before you would unload. At the paper mill they had what they called the Hot Pond. It was about thirty by fifty square feet where you would dump your load so they could be cleaned and moved to a conveyer and taken up into the mill. Well, you would pull up to the side of the pond and take off the load binder and the top chain that would wrap around the whole load to keep it in place during transit. Sometimes, when you would release the binder and release the side bunks on the load, the whole thing would just come crashing down. Imagine fifteen or twenty huge logs coming at you while you're standing right next to them on the ice. More than one life was lost that way. Other times, the logs would be wedged together so that when you took the chains off you'd have to take a cant hook and try to pry them apart. Another really hazardous job to test your agility; when that load lets go, you better be prepared to make tracks, and fast.

The whole thing about that operation is that you're dealing with such tremendous weight, and at that time there wasn't any mechanized equipment to deal with it, as there is now. I can't imagine how many twelve-ply truck tires were blown out every month. We used to keep 90 P.S.I. of air in them and when they popped it was like being in Hiroshima in 1945. However, I think the majority of people in our area of Michigan owe whatever success they have at least in part to lumberjacks and homesteaders who pioneered that area at the turn of the century. There is still a lot of woods work but it is done by so few people compared to the Pine and Hemlock days, and so commercialized that it is a forgotten part of our past for the most part.

The Workers

We will talk some about the lumberjacks themselves. Everyone had his own way and his own story if you could get them to talk about themselves. Often, they pretty much kept to themselves and did their jobs without saying anything other than what they needed to in order to do their work. In a camp like ours, every man had a nickname that he answered to. Many were quite funny and you wondered how they came about. A few I remember are Whiskey Bill, Lame George, Three-Finger Carlson, Eggy Mike, Ivan Ruskie, Pork Chop, and Farmer. One had a limp and was called "Step and a half." Others were Cigar, Little Hill, Happy Jack, Carpenter Matt, One-Wing Frank (had one arm), Ridge Rat, and many more. It seemed no one was called by their actual name. There was Harry, my friend who I had worked with for over a year and knew well. He often asked me if I went to school. I said, "Of course I did."

One day after supper (I stayed at the camp sometimes if my car was not running or if the weather was too bad),

Harry said, "I'm going to the horse barn and take care of the team. Come down there, I need to talk to you." At first I was kind of reluctant, but he was such a good friend, although tough as nails and willing to fight at the drop of a hat if anyone provoked him. So after I fueled my truck and checked the oil, tires, etc., I walked over. As I entered the horse barn, he came over with a handful of unopened letters in his hand.

I said, "What's going on, Harry?"

He handed me a letter and said, "Read me that son of a bitch." Here he had about three months of mail and he didn't want anyone to know he couldn't read.

I said, "Why didn't you tell me a long time ago? I'd have gladly done that for you."

He said, "They don't give a damn about me and only write for money, anyway, so I don't care if I read them or not."

The letters were from his family in Wisconsin, and one from a sister. She said how much she loved him. As I was reading, he kept saying, "Bullshit. She never cared for anyone but herself." Also, she wrote that she was hoping he would come home for the summer so they could spend time together. "She can go to hell. I'd rather stay here by myself when the camp closes." It's hard to understand people like that. Maybe it's the life they live, I guess.

There was a "Rudy" (Russian) who was another odd sort. He always wore Bib Overalls and never talked or bothered anybody. He never went anywhere, and when the camp closed he asked if he could stay there as a caretaker, so he really never left. One day we were sawing a big Tamarack when all at once he stopped. I said, "What's wrong?"

He said, "How much do you want for your car?" I told him I didn't care to sell it. He said, "I'll pay cash. I have a lot of money." I kind of smiled and told him I wasn't interested. He persisted and said, "I'll show you I have the money." He reached into his overalls and pulled out a thousand dollars. I wonder how long he saved that, working for less than one dollar an hour.

My January Vacation

It was early January 1947 when my friend Chubby and I were talking one day about not having a decent paying job and we were just spinning our wheels and maybe we should try something else. We both had saved a few dollars and discussed making a trip to Detroit; surely we'd find something to do there. At least there were places to look for work which we didn't have here. The more we talked, we convinced ourselves we had nothing to lose.

I had just stuck a new engine in my Model A and it ran like a top, so we said, "Let's do it".

For whatever reason, we left at 7:30 in the evening. I remember it well: it was 24° below zero and snowing. I had everything I thought we'd need (shovel, tire chains, tools, spare 5 gallon can of gas) because those days in the UP we didn't have 24 hour service stations. With our suitcases, bag of lunch, etc. the back seat was jammed full.

We were all wound up and everything was going well. The snow was only about 8" on the road and it appeared to be stopping. We were making about 40 m.p.h., which was good. We got about half way from Greenland to Baraga (about 25 miles from home) when we had the first problem. There was a real sharp hair pin curve and when we got to it, here comes a car around the corner in my lane. There wasn't anything to do but hit the ditch or have a head-on.

It came up so fast there wasn't time to try to stop. We went about a whole car length into the snow bank. I had to exit through the window; the snow was almost to the roof. We only had one shovel so we took turns shoveling and about 1:30 in the morning we got back on the road. The other driver never stopped; he probably knew what would happen if he had.

We made it to Marquette without trouble and found one filling station open. The owner said we should wait until morning to go on because from there to St. Ignace it was going to be impossible to get gas or help if we had trouble. He had another 5 gallon can so we had quite a lot of gas, but it started snowing again.

It continued all night and we were plowing deep ruts now. We got about 60 miles from St. Ignace along the Lake Michigan shore when all at once we got a flat tire. We were about twenty feet from the water with a strong wind coming in. I don't know what the wind chill would have been but I've never felt so cold.

We put the spare on after cleaning a spot and finding the jack under all of our junk. The spare wasn't too good so after we got underway (by now it was almost daylight) I stopped at the first station we came to and told him to patch the tire and put it on the car and return the spare to its place.

Once again we got underway but the car was bouncing and shaking. I thought we had another flat but everything looked fine so we drove on. After about 25 miles I told Chub, "We'd better put that old spare on, I think there's something wrong with that tire we had repaired," so we did.

(When we got to Detroit I had the tire taken down in a gas station to find out what was wrong with it. Well, he broke it down and found a two cell flashlight between the casing and inner tube. The other man must have been looking for a nail and left it in the tire.)

We got to the ferry at St. Ignace and it was the first one to leave the dock since midnight. The channel was frozen solid and it took almost 5 hours to cross. They would back up and take a run and pick up about 40 feet, then do it again.

We were like a yo-yo but finally got off and on our way again. The weather was better and not so much snow so it was better driving. A while later the Model A started slowing down and wouldn't go over 30 m.p.h. I couldn't imagine what was wrong. I stopped and checked the gas-line thinking it might be beginning to freeze but it was clear. I stopped around Gaylord and had a Ford garage check it. He said he'd never seen anything like that so I drove all the way to Detroit at 30 m.p.h.

I later had my friend Hugo look at it. He owned a Texaco station. I had never had this problem before but he had the car up on the hoist and discovered that I had hit the muffler on a chunk of ice and dented it blocking the air flow. He took a chisel and made a hole through the middle of it and it worked fine.

As it turned out, Chub and I got a room and applied for a job near the rooming house. We got hired at the Plymouth assembly plant on Lynch Road. We were both on the line and worked near each other. Everything was working out perfectly except we were putting out 90 cars an hour and we had to run for eight hours. If a bolt didn't go on right or the threads were stripped or anything then you really had to go to catch up.

Also, after a few days, the place we had the room at had the devil's grandmother for caretaker. She was a real bitch. We stayed about 10 days and one day on the way to work I asked Chub if he'd had enough. He said, "I've been hoping you'd ask that for many days now." So we quit. We were both so disillusioned we didn't even look for another job or place to live. We loaded up and started home.

This time we had a better trip. The sun was out and the car ran like a deer. We got to the ferry about dark and thought about getting a motel but everything was going so well we decided to drive right through.

We had forgotten to fill our gas cans and after the last gas station we were running on empty about 4 A.M. U.S.2 is a very lonely road on a January freezing night; not a sign of life or cars on the road either. Finally we came to a little house on the side of the road with a gas pump in front so I stopped. I knocked on the door but no answer so I went around back and started pounding on the door. A man's voice finally yelled, "We're closed. Get the hell out of here." I explained that it's 25 below zero, my gauge reads zero and when the engine dies so will we. He finally calmed down and said," I'll be out in a few minutes" which he did. He filled my tank and cans and we both thanked him many times.

He had a little showroom with oil and antifreeze, also his desk and a small table. He started to explain why he was so angry with us. He said there was a head on accident right in front of his place a few hours earlier; a real bad one. Another car happened to come by at the same time and a Doctor was driving it. He said they carried one man in and they operated on him on the table there but couldn't save him. He pulled a cardboard box out from under the table and said, "Look, here's his legs." I had been kind of tired but I was wide awake the rest of the way home after that.

I went back to my old job in the lumber camp and stayed there until September of '47 when our whole family moved to Detroit. We've never lived in the U.P. since and only go up on vacations now. All of our old neighbors and relatives are gone now and there is a new generation making their mark on Ontonagon soil.

The Bus Trip

When World War II began, the Selective Service System was put in motion immediately and every man from eighteen years of age to thirty-eight was on the list. Our town was so small and there weren't that many boys in that area, so when their names were called up they got their greetings. That was a letter that began, "Greetings from the President of the United States of America, etc. etc." It was a classification telling you exactly where you stood in the draft procedure. The ones who were 1-A were given a time, date, and location where to report for a pre-induction physical examination. Then, if we passed, we were then given a date when and where to report for basic training.

Well when our little village received our greetings it was a major news event because they called up fifty boys the first time, in a county that had a total population of about 1200. That was arguably the major part of the young males in town. Of course, everyone feared the start of the war, but, because they were all very patriotic, these kids were already heroes just for making the list. As much as their families were hurt by having their sons leaving for who knows where to fight and possibly die, the people of our village were very proud of them.

When the draft in the early '40s was in full swing, just about every eligible man went into the service. At home, only minors and older men were around, and all the rest were gone. There are many stories to tell about everything being rationed. Today we have a gas shortage, but in the '40s we were allowed four gallons a-week. The average car like the Ford A got about nine or ten miles per gallon, so it was hard.

Back to the bus trip. There weren't any places in the
Upper Peninsula of Michigan where young recruits could
have their physicals, so a Greyhound bus was sent to take
them to Milwaukee, Wisconsin to be examined. They
returned home after a couple of days, then had fifteen days to
get their things in order and report for induction. Most of the
guys from our area went to Camp McCoy in Wisconsin for
training or re-assignment to other camps around the country.

Well, the date to leave was set and the Greyhound
would be on Main Street at 10:00 A.M. on Wednesday. The
men were all warned to be sure to be on time or face an
A.W.O.L. charge, which could result in prison time. All
these farm boys wanted to do everything right so they all
came at about 7 A.M. to make sure they weren't late, most of
them with their families.

Jim's Bar was right in the middle of town, right where
the bus was to leave from, so, wanting to show these brave
young boys a good time, Jim talked to the sheriff and told
him the plan. The sheriff said he'd look the other way and
stay home until the bus had left. The kids began to gather and
Jim came out and said they were all welcome and the drinks
were free all morning. A lot of the kids had never tried the
hard stuff before, and of course the ones who did rushed in to
celebrate. The place was like a beehive for a couple hours
until the bus pulled up in front of the bar. Needless to say, by
10:45 everyone in the place was shit-faced. Some were
singing, some were just walking around in a daze. Jim stood
by the door when they all filed out. He shook their hands,
wished them well, and gave each a bottle of whiskey to take
on the bus. Bruno was kind of the town drunk, and of course
Walter carried him out to the bus. Bruno had crapped in his

pants but they couldn't leave him so on he went. The parents and loved ones cried and said their goodbyes. The big diesel came to life and slowly began to move, a big cloud of blue smoke coming from its stack. As it got underway, about fifteen hands appeared out the windows on both sides of the bus, each holding a bottle of booze. A woman was heard to say, "Heaven help us," as the bus disappeared down Route 45, headed south to Milwaukee.

The bus was set to return on Saturday, around 6 P.M., so the crowd was there waiting to take everyone home. Sure enough, right on time it rolled up in front of Jim's bar. The bus rumbled to a stop in a cloud of blue smoke and dust, the air brakes hissing until it stopped moving. The door opened and the driver came out and kicked an empty bottle out of the doorway. He looked disheveled and his face was as white as snow. He said, "I can't believe we made it back."

Next, after a few minutes, came Walter, carrying Bruno who had his shit pants on. No one knew if it was the same one as when he left or if it was a new batch. He was barely awake and he looked bad: vomit all over his shirt, his eyes looking like two piss holes in a snow bank. He looked up and said, "When are we going to get to Milwaukee?"

Walter just said, "Shut up and go lay down by that building."

After everyone was off and most had left to go home, Ray decided to stay in Jim's Bar and talk to a couple of the boys that had been on the bus. They all talked and laughed about a few things that had happened. One of the boys said that when they got there the first thing they had to do was to fill out a form asking about their past – where they lived, worked, etc. He said he peeked over at Eero who was filling out the part about occupation. Eero had put, "I saw logs and count them."

Then, during the physical, they were lined up in front of a door and were let in one at a time. There was nothing in the room except a Sergeant sitting at a desk. They were all undressed, and when it was Lawrence's turn to go in, the Sergeant said, "Turn your back to me, bend over, and spread your cheeks." Well, Lawrence bent over, he put both hands to his mouth and with both forefingers, spread his mouth open. Another kid came in and when he bent over the Sergeant said, "Boy, you sure got a dirty ass."

The kid said, "That's probably because I been shitting out of it for nineteen years now." Quite an exam!

One of the other doctors in Milwaukee told the men that he'd been a doctor all his life, and never had he seen so many men with heart problems.

Anyway, after all was said, most everyone passed and went into the service. There were very few classified Four F, meaning not eligible. We had one neighbor who had five sons in the service. One of them didn't come back. There were quite a few others who were lost also. We had another neighbor who had a son who was pretty mentally lacking, so when he got his greetings letter, his father took him to town to the draft board and said, "Here he is if you want him."

The official asked, "Where do you live?"

The boy, Gus, who had a bad habit of stuttering, answered, "H-H-H-How m-m-m-many c-cows do the Makis have?"

The man said, "Take him home."

The Government Pole

There were two rivers, both about a mile from our house in each direction, and they were our main form of recreation. In the winter we would shovel the snow off the ice and make a big rink, build a bonfire, and spend the evening. Also, the high river banks were covered with snow and made excellent sledding trails. We could stay for hours in the -10 degree weather and really enjoy ourselves.

In the spring we had smelt runs and all summer long we'd fish, nearly every evening. None of us had any rods or reels. We'd get some line and a hook and attach them to a maple tree six or seven feet long. That was known as a "government pole." I think we caught as many fish as anyone else and the worms were free.

Also in the spring spawning season, the pike and especially the suckers could be netted by the dozens. We'd get a wash tub full in a half hour on a good night. My grandfather would get a pile of fish and dig a hole in the ground and bury them. After a time, he would dig them up and use the rotten fish for bait on his coyote traps. They were excellent lures, he said.

The Shining Light

When our house was sold, I only took two things as souvenirs. One was the leg-hold traps I used to catch weasels. I only had one trap and it took me nearly one season to make enough to buy another. I have them both hanging in my shed and every day I have memories of those cold, -20 degree mornings going out to see my trap on skis before school. Then I had two! I couldn't wait to get out after that. Things were certainly looking up. We'd get on the bus and all the kids would ask, "Get anything?" The business wasn't very lucrative but boy I sure felt important.

The other thing I brought home I never gave much thought, but I was sitting in my studio painting a picture of a farm, and contemplating the composition. I began to gaze at my kerosene lantern which I have on my desk. I thought, what a life-saving fixture we had. It seemed so insignificant when I threw it in the trunk of my car at the time. I didn't know what people would have done without a lantern. We had a kerosene lamp in our kitchen but we had to milk the cows, feed them, and do all the chores before daylight and after dark. We hung the lantern on a pole in the barn and lighted our way to the haystack, water pump, sauna, etc. We often had to bring wood into the house after dark, and at night it was **dark**. And, of course, everyone uses the outhouse. There were no flashlights, so what would you do? If company came over and stayed after dark, you offered them your lantern. What a lifesaver. Before we had electricity I didn't know how one could live without it.

The R.E.A. (Rural Electric Administartion) didn't come to our area until 1937 and, like Thomas Kinkade said,

"We lighted up the world." It's hard now to imagine not having electricity – all our appliances, tools, etc., are taken for granted. But, when you think of doing everything by hand, it would seem impossible to get along without electricity. My mother used to heat her curling iron by dangling it through the chimney of our Kerosene lamp so the end of the iron would be over the flame. And, when she ironed clothes, the irons were heated on top of the wood stove in the kitchen. Our neighbors had a blacksmith shop and when he needed to make a hole through a piece of lumber, rather than drilling it by hand, he would heat a steel rod on the forge until it was white hot, then poke a hole in a few seconds. They always found a way. He also had a water pump in his barn with which he watered 25 head of cattle and the horses. The troughs for both sides of the barn had to be filled by carrying many pails to supply all the animals – no problem. He took a couple of old Model T inner tubes from the tires, cut them in half, tied one end to the pump, the other to the trough. Now all the labor needed was to man the pump. I never remember seeing a water hose in those early days. If there were any, people probably couldn't afford one.

If there were any problems they always found a way. One old Finnish farmer had his barn roof cut out with about a ten-foot gap in it. He built an inclined driveway up both sides of the barn and would drive his horses up with a load of hay. He could fill the barn much easier than pitching it up from ground level. When we were in Finland, we saw many barns built that way.

Cupping

The last time we met, Wayne and I were talking about the old days and customs and I asked if he had ever heard of the art of cupping. He said no, and later I asked a number of other older people I grew up with and none of them ever remembered hearing of it either. I thought I'd add it in here along with the rest of these stories because it's such an unusual home health remedy.

It can be found on the computer with a little different application. I mentioned it to our family doctor and even he had never heard of it being performed this way, although he said he had medical books from college explaining the purpose of this lost art.

The Finns all had a sauna and when the person doing the procedure came, they would heat up the steam room as hot as they could stand. When in a sauna, your veins come up near the surface of your skin. He would take a cows horn and place it on a vein on your leg, shoulder, or wherever the sore spot was and suck on the horn and get it even nearer the surface. Then he took a razor blade and made about ten small incisions on the vein until the blood ran freely for a few minutes. Then, when you left the steam room the vein would recede and the razor marks would stop bleeding. They claimed this would flush out the veins, and especially in the legs where the heart couldn't pump all of the blood back, there was always a small residue left. Hence the blood letting. It would clear it all out and relieve the aches and pains.

Another funny thing happened when I was a kid. Hardly anyone had a family doctor, so if you had problems you either took home remedies or lived with it, unless it was just unbearable. One day, a man went house to house asking if anyone needed a massage. Well, it so happened our neighbor was suffering with a real sore back. He asked how much it would cost for a treatment and the man replied, "I'm sure I could help you with your problem and I hate to turn you down, but I've made it a practice to only massage women. I don't do men at all." Ha! Ha!

Uncle Ed's Fiction

Stalking Big Eli

The ice-cold wind was blowing, there was a light snow in the air and daylight was breaking as the old man started his hike up the muddy, rutted logging road that led into the woods. His pace was in slow measured steps and his whole body ached with his every step. His body rebelled as he made his way through the tall dead grass and mud, being careful not to step into the deep ruts covered with snow. He pulled his cap over his ears, his hands freezing despite the gloves.

He had his 30-30, which had joined him on these hunting trips for over fifty years. It was like a fine tuned watch and a lifelong friend who he cradled like a mother caressing her child as he carefully made his way further into the snow covered forest. The pine trees waved gently in the breeze and whispered their welcome from beneath their layer of white. The old man was reminded of his past deer hunting experiences and thought of the many deer he had stalked and lessons he had learned.

He moved slowly for patience was his greatest virtue. If he persisted in his plan he knew success would surely follow. The one reason he was apprehensive was the phantom buck he had seen and hunted every season for the last five years. This one was like no other in that it would seldom offer more than a glimpse of itself before disappearing into the forest. Although he had tried every hunting tactic he had ever learned, he could not seem to get a good look at this huge animal. He estimated it to be at least

18 points and 290 pounds. It was no wonder it had never been caught. This animal was so wily and elusive no man could ever catch sight of it! Through his years of experience, he knew the old, wise ones never came near human habitat during daylight hours. The only chance was to go where no other hunter would venture, deep into the swamp and beaver dam areas.

He paused to rest for a moment and to contemplate his plan of action. The wind had settled down now as the large snowflakes fell silently to earth. At the top of the ravine where he stood he could observe the valley below and thought what a beautiful sight was this God's creation. A few last aspen leaves finally lost their hold and fluttered down like confetti during a celebration. In the white silence, he heard the call of the loon alerting all creatures that it was dawn and time to come out of hiding.

He began to feel a chill and stood up painfully, looking for an opening in the briar patch so he could continue on his way. He checked his compass to see that he was still on course heading toward the large beaver dam in his path. He reasoned that the one he called "Big Eli" would find a small island in the underwater area and lay there all day undisturbed until twilight when he would come out to feed. The dam was about a mile across so he knew it would be an ordeal. The old wise ones wouldn't bed down unless it was an absolutely secluded spot where they could see in all directions.

Finally the area he looked for began to appear; there were downed trees all crisscrossed showing beaver activity and a small stream that quickly grew into a swamp with water a foot deep as far as the eye could see. Again he hesitated, the biting cold making his knees and back condition worsen. If he entered this domain of ice and water, it most certainly was going to be a long cold trek with no certainty of success, but he was convinced it was the only way he could have any chance of seeing a deer of respectable size.

His watch now showed 7:30. Surely they were all soon headed for their beds so he stepped out into the frozen water and slowly began making his way to the center. He estimated the spot to be nearly a mile away. It was slow going and sometime the water got too deep, which forced the old man to backtrack and find another route. The cold was numbing, but he kept moving and slowly progressed through the woods and stumps, keeping watch in every direction. He watched every pine tree in case there were deer sleeping under their branches. Occasionally he would notice a high knoll sticking out of the water, which he knew made for great bedding spots. Many times in the past he had been out smarted by a white tail leaping right in front of him because he was more focused on where he stepped as opposed to the terrain ahead.

Half an hour passed; he had worked his way far into the swamp with no sign of Big Eli. Had he miscalculated? Should he turn back? His cold feet were stinging and his rifle seemed to weigh a ton. The water was beginning to freeze which made his every step louder and louder. For a moment he considered giving up, but he kept pressing onward. His reasoning was that he could be within yards of getting to see the big one who had filled his thoughts for the last five years.

It was only minutes later when he heard a huge snort and suddenly a loud crashing sound ahead. The panicked deer had smashed headlong through the water and brush to escape the intruder. The old man didn't see the animal but knew from the sound this was no yearling. He got to the now vacant bed and was rewarded with one of the largest tracks he had ever seen. It had to be Big Eli.

As he looked for the broken ice to find and track the great one, his face lit up and with a toothless smile he said, "Let the hunt begin." Now all of his senses were alive, he no longer felt cold, his aches were gone, and his whole body felt like a finely tuned piano. Fifty years of experience now were pitted against this cagey competitor to see who would out-do the other.

It took him an hour to get through the swamp, but in the freshly fallen snow, he had no trouble following the unmistakable track of the elusive Eli. He didn't have any idea how far ahead it was as he followed the tracks straight ahead toward the river. Far in the distance he heard a squirrel begin to chatter incessantly who knew the intruder was going through his territory. In ten minutes, he too entered the same domain, and as he heard the chatter begin again, he knew he was getting closer.

He stood high on the riverbank and wondered if it would disappear into the thick brush or would he cross to the other side? The river was quite wide and some ice had formed along the banks. He thought Eli may not want to try and swim; rather, he could stay in the briars and sneak away knowing the man couldn't make headway doing the same.

He followed the track right to the river's edge. They went straight ahead and he could see the broken ice on the opposite shore where it had gone up the bank and over the ridge.

Now the old man had a problem. The only way to cross the river was to go one way or the other until there was a fallen tree or log making a bridge to the other side. He took off running to his right. There were thick briars near the water and they tore at his clothes. He ran about 200 yards and finally found a large, fallen hemlock lying across the river. It was covered with wet snow and ice. It would be treacherous to try and cross. He knew if he lost his balance he would come out soaked to the skin and the 10° weather would take its toll, if he were even able to survive at all. He thought for only a minute before climbing up on the log and slowly inching forward. He brushed the snow away at every step and was soon at the other side. What waited for him was a very steep embankment that tested the old man's climbing skills. He slipped back several times before making it to the top and facing a heavily wooded pine grove.

A heavy cluster of pine trees covered with snow is arguably the worst condition for hunting. Visibility is only a few feet in any direction no matter where you stand. He still had the tracks and knew Eli was close. The mighty deer had crossed through the pines for over an hour and knew the old man was close, so Eli headed for a large aspen wooded area.

The old man finally emerged from the pines and stayed on the trail for another hour without incident. He was growing tired and wondered how far behind he was. There was a fallen tree about fifty yards ahead near the ridge. He saw it and thought he'd stop and rest when he got there. His legs were hurting again, and his back began to ache as well. He carried a sandwich and had a thermos with some hot coffee. After a few minutes he would resume his hunt. He knew the great one had to be tired too, so he couldn't be too far behind.

He got up and resumed the search. Suddenly, something told him not to take another step. The old man stood completely still and surveyed the area ahead. He saw nothing, yet something told him to wait silently. Finally he saw a huge form silently disappear over the ridgeline ahead. He crept and looked over the hilltop, but the wise old one had only shown himself to let him know the game was still in progress and that the hunt would continue. There were several hours of daylight left so there was no rush, Eli would wait to taunt him again.

Through the slashing and logging roads they went. The old man never saw Eli, but the tracks indicated he was not far behind. He thought he had seen a glimpse of the huge antlers across the ravine, but that was all. He doggedly stayed behind, even though they were many miles from where the hunt had started.

Eli was going in a straight line through some aspen thickets when the tracks began a big sweeping turn to the left. When the old man saw the tracks turn, he knew immediately, from fifty years of experience, what to do next. When deer are tracked a long time they will tire, so they'll make a big turn and come back behind to their own trail to see if the hunter is still in pursuit. The old man made a sharp ninety degree turn to the left and ran as fast as his body would allow for about a hundred yards. He looked for a spot where the deer would cross so he could intercept it. He stepped into a thick briar patch near a small clearing to wait. He made sure his gun was ready and the safety off as he aimed it in the direction he thought Eli would come.

90

It was only about ten minutes when he heard the crashing sound coming toward him. He stood motionless for what seemed an eternity when he detected the beautiful specimen coming straight at him. His heart was pounding and he was even counting the points on his antlers. Eli slowly, cautiously entered the clearing and stopped…too late. Eli spotted the barrel of the rifle pointed at it from behind a windfall. Eli froze in his tracks and knew it was useless to run, he had no chance. The old man stepped out and there they stood, face to face. The deer held his magnificent head high and proudly stood there knowing he had lost the fight.

After a minute, the old man, with a tear in his eye, lowered the rifle. "It was a great hunt. Next year we'll do it again." The deer seemed to understand, nodded his head and turned to leave. Slowly Eli walked, stopped and looked back as if to say "Good-bye" as he disappeared into the brush.

As he walked back to his truck, the old man noticed how tired he was. His back and legs ached, but it was worth it. He only wished he'd had a camera to show his encounter with "The Great One". He unloaded his rifle, put it away and was about to enter his truck when he turned around to look back into the forest.

Standing in all his glory at the entrance of the forest was Eli. After one last look, Eli slowly turned and raised his white flag and slowly disappeared back into the woods. As the old man smiled and considered the day's events, it was as if Eli had seemed to say, "Good-bye old friend. Next year we'll try again."

Hunting and the Frozen Trunk

Toivo, Eino, and Urho went on their annual hunt for two weeks. They hunted hard and drank harder but had no success. Finally on the last day they decided that having seen nothing but Baldies (no horns) they would take a couple home for meat.

They bagged a couple, dressed them out, quartered them out and packed them in the trunk of their 1929 Chevy coupe.

As they boarded up the windows of the shack and shoveled out most of the debris it started to snow really hard. Eino said, "We better get going. It's a mile and a half to the main road and there's eight inches on the ground."

Taivo said, "Well when I loaded the trunk I put the irons on the tires and with 150 lbs. of meat in back we'll be OK."

They were all set so they locked up, got in the car cracked a six pack and started out. Everything went smoothly even though the snow was up to the headlights by the time they reached the highway.

As they rounded the last curve they spotted a D.N.R. truck blocking the exit, so there was no alternative except to stop. The game warden came over and said, "I knew you'd come out with this storm. Have you got anything illegal in your car?"

"No," said Eino, "we hunted hard but no luck."

"What do you have in the trunk?" the warden asked. "I'd like to take a look. I know you fellas from before and I don't think you'd go home empty handed."

"There isn't anything except our guns and clothes," argued Eino, but to no avail. He handed the agent the keys and said "Well, take the keys and open it if you have to," thinking they were doomed.

The officer took the key but the lock was frozen solid and try as he did, it wouldn't open. He even tried to heat it with a match but it wouldn't budge. Finally he gave up and said, "I really don't believe you but short of smashing your trunk I can't open it so I'll let you move on."

As they went on their way they chuckled, and Eino said, "I'll crack this last six pack, it's time to celebrate. I thought we were headed to the big house for sure. Cheers."

Taivo remarked, "Well, I knew we were OK because I knew the lock wouldn't open ...I pissed on it just before we left camp."

1936

Leaving Ontonagon, 1946

www.ingramcontent.com/pod-product-compliance
Lightning Source LLC
Chambersburg PA
CBHW031326040426
42443CB00005B/232